THE ASTROLOGY GUIDE

UNDERSTAND YOUR SIGNS FOR DATING,
FRIENDSHIPS, MONEY, AND SEX

TIMOTHY WELLS

INTRODUCTION

Are you ready to discover how your Astrology Sign relates to your love life, improving relationships, and a career that fits your personality? For thousands of years people have been using Astrology to determine which choices are best for him or her. This book will dive into all 12 astrological signs in-depth with regard to personality, love compatibility, and careers that fit best.

Astrology can lead to a better understanding of yourself, of your personal and professional relationships, and of how others perceive you. You are about to discover each signs:
- Positive and Negative Personality Traits
- How Much Money Will Be Earned
- How Your Relationship Will Turn Out
- How Romantic and Sexual Someone Is
- And Much More!

Enjoy!

The Personality Traits of Each Sign

The first question you might want to ask is "how does astrology determine your traits?" Each of the 12 zodiac signs has its ruling planet, and the characteristics of these planets govern your personality. Aside from a person's ruling planet, his element also has something to do with his traits as a whole. Astrologers rely on these factors to identify each zodiac sign's behaviors or attitudes.

Aries (March 21-April 20)

Aries, as the first sign in the zodiac, represents raw energy. Aries is symbolized by a young Ram that is energetic, adventurous, and enthusiastic. As someone full of energy, an Aries is lively by nature. He's the type who can lighten up a room whenever he's around. So if you're at a party with an Aries, expect him to be the one dancing around or chatting with his newly-met buddies. His element is fire while his ruling planet is Mars, that's why this sign is a very positive sign. An Aries has a deep need for action so it's only natural for this sign to always look for excitement in life.

Taurus (April 20-May 20)

Taurus, ruled by planet Venus and symbolized by the Bull, is practical and artistic. He is a generous and loyal individual who loves maintaining friendships as well as relationships. People can always count on Taurus with his dependable trait. He also likes to appear pleasant to people. And just like a bull, a Taurus can be stubborn at times, but he is fairly simple in many things like material things. When it comes to attaining his goals, Taurus can be a ball of fire with towering ambitions.

Gemini (May 21-June 20)

Gemini, or The Twins, is an Air sign. Just like all the other signs, Gemini also has distinguishing positive and negative traits. He is ever changing so immovability is not the word for Gemini. As an Air sign, the Gemini is adaptable to any given situation. He's more likely to become easygoing, and he's also very forgiving. Gemini is known as an intellectual sign so he always wants to be updated with what's going on around him whether it's news or gossips. Conversely, since he's characterized by The Twins, he has the possibility to be inconsistent or indecisive in life.

Cancer (June 21-July 22)

Cancer is a Water sign and is symbolized by The Crab. People who were born under this sign are known for being complex individuals. A Cancer is remarkably tender and spontaneous. He has a deep need for security in all facets of life. Illustrated by the Crab, Cancer easily get anxious, but that lack of confidence won't show because he tends to be mysterious and quiet. Generally, a Cancer is someone who loves to be at home and to nurture rapports. When it comes to making decisions, a Cancer will trust his gut feeling more than logic. Cancer is all about love; he loves people and he wants to be loved in return.

Leo (July 23- August 22)

A Leo, ruled by the Sun, is a very warm sign. He loves to be in the limelight and wants to be loved and admired by the crowd. Ruled by the sun, a Leo is self-expressive and authoritative. Leo, symbolized by the Lion, has a huge ego. He also is quick to become jealous as he is desirous by nature, and he can be a little bit controlling too. Still, his kindhearted nature makes a Leo stand out and shine.

Virgo (August 23-September 22)

Virgo, the Virgin, is the type whose waters run deep. Virgo is smart and intellectual. This sign is ruled by Mercury so he is naturally methodical and analytical. Nevertheless, Virgos want to believe that they are perfectionists, and that's why many Virgos make excellent managers. A Virgo is good at following instructions, too. However, it will be a tough job to blow away a Virgo as he always aim for perfection.

Libra (September 23-October 22)

Libra is an Air sign and is ruled by Venus. A Libra is known for being tactful, charming, and romantic. His life revolves around love as he is ruled by planet Venus. He is a lover of beauty, pleasure, and social life. He likes to please everybody. Generally, this sign is loved by others because of his fairness. A Libra has a strong sense of justice so he's not the type to bully or take advantage of others.

Scorpio (October 23-November 21)

Scorpio ruled by Pluto and is denoted by the Scorpion, is an enigmatic and strong-willed sign. A Scorpio is known for being persevering, especially when it comes to reaching his goals. He has his head on for every situation given that he's fearless and quite ambitious. He's also frank so he does not mind saying what's on his mind, even if he appears too intense.

Sagittarius (November 22-December 21)

A Sagittarius is led by Jupiter and signified by the Archer. He is optimistic and adventure-seeking. The Archer makes him a natural charmer, so it's no sweat for him to fascinate other people. He will be a good companion who always aims for escapade. He is physically-game for anything. Whenever a Sagittarius says something, he means it because he's straightforward by nature. However, he has an impulse to become tactless in handling things. He can be restless too at times, given that his energy isn't well-directed.

ONE

Capricorn (December 22-January 19)
Capricorn, represented by the Goat, is naturally stable and calm. People under this sign are ruled by planet Saturn. A Capricorn is known for being a practical individual as he uses a pragmatic approach before deciding on things. He is wise and sensible. People can rely on a Capricorn for valuable advice as he will not be afraid to tell them if they're doing things wrong. The Capricorn is a very motivated sign; once he aims for something, he'll patiently get it.

AQUARIUS (JANUARY 20-FEBRUARY 18)
Aquarius is under planet Uranus and Saturn, and symbolized by the water-bearer. People born under this sign are always up for excitement, so you'll see them making new friends or making others feel happy. Aquarius has a humanitarian attitude wherein he loves making the world a happy place. He's the type who likes helping others. People under this sign are also intelligent and inventive.

. . .

PISCES (FEBRUARY 19-MARCH **20**)

Pisces, the last sign of the zodiac is ruled by Neptune and is denoted by the Fish. He is a highly creative and imaginative individual. He can come up with innovative ideas that will help him reach greater heights. People born under this sign are compassionate so they always have a helping hand for those in need. However, they have sensitive souls that they tend to make mountain out of mole hills.

TWO

How Much Money Will You Make?

MONEY AND ASTROLOGY also comes hand in hand. Even if the stars and the planets won't literally give you gazillions of dollars from above, these elements still have a spell on your personality as a whole, including the way you handle money. When it comes to spending and managing finances, each sign also has different attitudes and beliefs. This chapter will give you an idea on how astrology works on the financial aspect of your life.

ARIES

An Aries-born is a driven individual so he could afford a cozy life. He has what it takes to earn a decent living. He can use his mind to get what he wants. However, he can be unruly at times so he has to be careful when it comes to impulse-buying, this is especially true for Aries women. For instance, an Aries is prone to getting unnecessary items at a grocery store at the last minute. To avoid hassles like this, Aries could use his mental ability to determine whether he really needs to buy something or not; or he could just bring along a friend who's wise at spending money.

Taurus

Taurus is practical so he does not actually have headaches when it comes to proper spending. But Taurus has to be on the watch over his laziness at times, as it could be a hindrance on attaining financial freedom. What's great about Taurus is that he'll save money to buy the things he wants. But, Taurus also has a tendency to indulge himself so much that it will be a test at times to handle money. The good thing about Taurus is that he is a savvy-shopper so he aims for the highest quality stuff with the lowest price.

THREE

Gemini

Gemini is the type who can easily create money, thanks to his crafty attitude. For an instance, he can use his talent to make a sale. But he has the weakness to become juvenile in handling it. For an example, Gemini will rather use his money to buy a plane ticket for fun than pay the bills. He can be immature when it comes to money; and That's why it's best for a Gemini to be with someone who can practically handle finances. As long as he's with someone who can manage their finances, Gemini will constantly be on the right track.

CANCER

Like Gemini, making money comes easily to Cancer-born individuals. But they differ when it comes to spending. Instead of spending their money for fun, Cancer will use it for investment. These people like to see how their finances grow. For Cancer, money defines his status in life. Still, he likes to use money to help other people. He is not really greedy, in fact, he wants to utilize money to reach out to others who are in need. Since Cancer has a deep need for security, he always wants to know that his money is safe. For Cancer-born people, money should be taken care of as it gives them a sense of supremacy.

Leo

Leo, as a fire sign, is extravagant. He wants the best of everything—cars, homes, and vacations to name a few. He won't settle for anything less. These people rely on money to appear dominant and presentable to the public. But making money is not an issue with Leo as this sign and money come hand in hand. For a Leo, money symbolizes hard work. So whenever a Leo wants something, he'll work really hard to get what he wants.

VIRGO

As someone who's apt at organizing things, Virgo can also manage his finances very well. For him, money is a serious matter so you'll rarely see him wasting it. Because he tends to worry a lot, he likes to save money for the future. Virgos do not like to depend on others financially so they are not likely to borrow money from others. But in general, they have a great skill at budgeting. They are also not avid spenders because they believe that money should be spent wisely.

LIBRA

Libra, represented by the Scales, is good at balancing things so he sees money as both valuable and practical. These people love money as they are after convenience. But more than that, they like to use money for their convenience. Once a Libra finds a job he really likes, he will put in extra work to succeed in it. Thus, Libra has to look for a job that will require his own sense of pace.

SCORPIO

Scorpio is another sign which is good at handling money. For him, it enhances his sense of freedom as well as security. It is very important for them that they think it will unlock every aspect of the world. Scorpio will likely use his power to get what he wants. That is why Scorpio will do a great job as a market analyst. Many people born under this sign usually get wiser in handling money as they grow older.

SAGITTARIUS

Instead of acquiring money, this sign's true desire is to be unique individuals. As a fire sign, Sagittarius is fun to be around and just enjoy spending cash. They use their money to please the people they love or to explore new things. However, even if they use money as a way of life, these people are not over spenders. They have a plan of how to use their finances well.

CAPRICORN

Capricorns are meticulous and cautious when it comes to handling money. They are more likely to attain financial stability because of their organized and disciplined characteristic. Rather than spending it lavishly, Capricorns will save whatever money they have so they can be used for more important things. They just need to find a stable job that will help them reach their financial goals; because once a Capricorn is motivated, everything else will be a piece of cake.

AQUARIUS

People born under Aquarius are serious about money, but they don't see it on the top of their priority list. Because they want to make the world a better place, Aquarius will do what's right with or without money. Since they are busy people who love looking for their mission here on Earth, Aquarius are advised to take things easy, especially when it comes to budgeting. Most of the time, they are too busy with other things that they tend to overlook budgeting their finances. When it comes to buying things, Aquarius can use his great thinking ability to look for quality items that are worth their penny.

PISCES

Pisces, the last of all signs, is more likely to daydream what he wants, like a car or a home that he really likes. However, they are intuitive when it comes to money so they can sense whether a business deal is going to be good or bad. Pisces, when it comes to marriage, will not have a hard time with finances as he knows how to choose a partner who's financially well-off. One advice for Pisces is to take a good dose of reality as this sign's dreamy spirit often misleads him from the reality of life.

HOW WILL YOUR RELATIONSHIPS BE?

ASTROLOGY DOES HAVE its own analysis when it comes to relationships. The Sun signs, as well as our elements have something to do with compatibility, so you might want to know which signs go are best for each other. Our ruling planets will tell us how.

ARIES

Aries loves meeting people but he prefers having a few close and long-term friends. An Aries can be the most entertaining, charming, and energetic friend one could ever have. In general, he is loyal and generous to his friends. But Aries has to be cautious about his short temper as he can be pushy or even bossy if it's the other way around. As children, Aries-born individuals are very affectionate to their parents.

Taurus

Taurus will be your most loyal friend once you won his trust. At first, Taurus will appear very shy and quiet, but once he grows comfortable with you, you'll find a true friend in him. Taurus children, can be stubborn at times, so for parents with a Taurus child, shower him with love and always exert great amount of patient in dealing with their tantrums.

Gemini

Gemini is a very likeable and entertaining friend. When it comes to a group of friends, a Gemini will not be afraid to become the center of attention. He's always up for fun and you can talk to him about almost anything. Their optimistic attitude is one of many reasons why people love Gemini. In general, these people are light-hearted so expect pleasant times whenever you're with a Gemini.

CANCER

Cancer is a lovable and sweet friend. They like to socialize, but they are not considered as the life of the party because they are quite shy. Instead of chatting and meeting new friends, they rather observe curiously at a party. When it comes to relationships, Cancer needs tons of love and affection because they have the tendency to become overly sensitive and moody. They can also be very insecure once they don't feel that they are not valued by others.

On the other hand, a Cancer child has a very wide imagination. So if you're a parent of a Cancer child, expect lots of creativity and daydreaming from him. As a parent, a Cancer will be very caring to his children especially if they are in bad taste. Cancer is also good at protecting his loved ones from harm. His mightily nurturing character draws him towards parenthood and family life.

Leo

Just like their fellow fire sign Aries, Leo only has a few close friends but he is not afraid to become the life of a party. In fact, a Leo loves attention. Typically, Leo is warm-hearted and generous. But Leo has to be extra careful when it comes to their tendencies to become bossy at times.

VIRGO

A Virgo is enjoyable to be around. Though he's more of an intellectual person, he can be quite funny and cheerful. Virgos are smart individuals, so when it comes to giving valuable pieces of advice, a Virgo will not disappoint because they will be honest and straightforward with you. Virgo can easily get along with water signs such as Scorpio and Cancer.

LIBRA

People born under this sign are sociable and lovely. Because they are represented by the Scales, Libra has a strong sense of justice. With this, they will find it hard to understand bullies and aggressive people. They get along very well with air signs like Aquarius and Gemini.

SCORPIO

In spite of their intense characteristics, people will find Scorpio fascinating and quite funny. This sign will get along best with water signs like Cancer and Pisces. Scorpio is a bit complex; so even if they appear sociable and too polite to a person, that doesn't mean that he treats him as his friend. The good thing about Scorpio is that he's loyal to the people he considers his true friends.

. . .

SAGITTARIUS

These people are generous and kind as friends. They prefer having companions on their quests. In general, they make wonderful companions. In marriage, a Sagittarius woman will stay honest to his spouse no matter what. She'll also be a great mother as she'll give her children independence more than strict supervision. Meanwhile, a Sagittarius father will love bonding with his children and will always forgive them.

CAPRICORN

Capricorn can be the most loyal and supportive friend you could ever have, as long as you show kindness and patience with him. Tight-knit Venus will make Capricorn love his friends even more. They aim for practicality and stability so you need to earn their trust first before they can call you their closest companions.

AQUARIUS

An Aquarius' water-bearing sign makes him engage to the concept of friendship. He is a warm and affectionate, so if you have an Aquarius friend, you'll surely not have any dull or awkward moments. This air sign loves adventure, conversation, and entertainment. There's so much rolling around in his head that he'll make interesting discussions. As a spouse, Aquarius is not prone to cheating, especially if he is happy with his marriage. Though, he's not the type who'll be staying at home most of the time. He likes to get busy with his career.

. . .

PISCES

This sign makes a great friend, but he can be easily thwarted if his friend isn't perfect. Pisces is very similar to Cancer, who is kind, sentimental, and sensitive. These two water signs will get along well, it is actually ideal for Scorpio and Pisces to become friends as Pisces will not be wretched by Scorpio's intense ways.

FOUR

Which Signs Are Most Compatible?

WHICH SIGNS ARE MOST compatible with each other? And which signs are more likely to have relationship conflicts? Astrology won't answer why a Gemini and Cancer couple broke up, for an instance but it does have some explanations on their personalities when it comes to love. This chapter will reveal your compatibility with other Sun signs.

ARIES

Aries is a positive and dominant sign. It means he craves lots of attention. With a fellow Aries, he will be able to build friendships and even love. But he has to overcome a bit of obstacles in the long run because the relationship will lack emotional stability. Aries is compatible to Leo because both are fire signs. Still, these two have to compromise because both of them have the tendencies to dominate each other. Aside from Leo and a fellow Aries, an Aries is also compatible with Libra, Sagittarius, and Gemini.

Taurus

Taurus likes a traditional set-up when it comes to marriage. It should start with sweet proposal, followed by a cozy wedding ceremony, then a romantic honeymoon. As they are represented by the Bull, Taurus-born individuals prefer simple occasions as long as they have their loved ones joining them. When it comes to compatible signs, Taurus goes best with a Capricorn, a Scorpio, and a Virgo. Taurus men and women do not like partners who flirt easily as they are quite possessive when it comes to love.

Gemini

Gemini is represented by The Lovers in the Tarot deck. It means they are rational, even when it comes to relationships. But since Gemini is an Air sign, he's not really after commitment. When it comes to love, Gemini needs lots of space and freedom as he's independent by nature. Though he is up for games, he does not play with his own heart. Gemini will prefer someone he can consider as a friend than just a lover. Gemini will get along very well with an Aquarius, an Aries, and a Sagittarius.

CANCER

Cancer-born people are conservative, sensitive, and shy so you don't expect them to make the first move. A Cancer is cautious in love but once he feels he can trust you, he will give himself unreservedly. He is quite mysterious too, so it will be a challenge to get to know him deeper. But once he found the one and truly fell in love, he will shower his partner with love and affection. This sign is most compatible with a Scorpio, Capricorn, Virgo, or Pisces. These signs, when joined by Cancer, will make a romantic and lasting bond.

Leo

Leo is the natural sign or love and romance. Leo romance is played out with high drama and passion. You are an ideal lover and are generous, ardent, appealing, and glamorous. Leo is possessive and loyal. Leo marries well below him and has the ardor and the passion to make the mate happy.

VIRGO

Virgo is particular, practical and realistic rather than romantic. Virgos are slow-burning fuses when it comes to lovemaking. Once, properly ignited, situations can lead to explosions that take some time to cool down. They're very fussy or demanding and critical of the personal habits of others, which can be a turn-off and can make it challenging for them to achieve a fulfilling relationship.

You are devoted and willing to serve their mates. You open up only to trusted confidants or long-time friends whom they can trust. If Virgos are in a committed relationship, and someone shows interest in their partner, it can spark a spout of jealousy.

. . .

LIBRA

For the Libra, love is much about beauty. Libra values aesthetics, symmetry, and harmony. This may be a problem for Libra because he may fail to appreciate the deeper meaning of love. He often takes a lot of time in deciding who is the perfect match for him, as he wants his mate to be balance in everything. Libras rarely have problems finding admirers and lovers, for their charm and elegance takes them far. Libra's know when they've fallen in love and like the romance of wine, candles, pink hearts and roses.

SCORPIO

Scorpio is a water sign, so it is known to be an emotional sign. When it comes to love, you feel it quite deeply. You can be very introspective and very emotionally driven. When you are in love, you can feel it right down to your core. This emotion is inseparable from the rest of your earthly existence. Often, the sensation of love defines you.

SAGITTARIUS

To the Sagittarius, love is a romantic adventure to be enjoyed and explored without feeling tied down. You will not hesitate to show your true feelings, and prefer your partner to stimulate and amuse you, and enjoy your company. You love to be touched and cuddle, and a big warm hug makes you feel wanted.

CAPRICORN

Capricorn, as an Earth sign, may seem reserved the first

meeting him. It's just that he carefully select the people who enter his life. Once you won a Capricorn's trust, you'll see his sharp and outgoing personality. However, Capricorn will choose his career over romance, because he believes that he's married to his job.

AQUARIUS

When it comes to relationships, Aquarius is very independent. He's also intellectual by nature. It's the reason why you'll rarely see him spend too much time on emotional situations. But once he is truly committed, he'll be a perfect lover who can give everything to his loved one. He'll shower his lover with all the affection he needs. This sign is most compatible with fellow air signs Libra and Gemini.

PISCES

Pisces will be very caring and sensual when it comes to his partner. He knows what to say and do to make his lover happy. He'll be ideal for earth signs Virgo, Taurus, and Capricorn as Pisces together with these signs will build stable and practical relationships. He can also have harmonious relationship with fellow water signs Cancer and Scorpio. With these water signs, Pisces will find lovers with the same intuition and emotions.

FIVE

Psychology & Astrology

IN PSYCHOLOGY, the main concern is the behaviors of an individual—how he acts and how he thinks. Now, does astrology contribute in the way a person thinks or feels? This chapter will reveal how the stars and the ruling planets influence our way of thinking, too.

ARIES
Aries trusts nobody. He likes living on his own. He lives a life with no regrets so he won't listen to other people who tell him what he should do. An Aries is known for putting down every criticism thrown to him whether it is positive or negative. An Aries is solid and will not simply change his mind.

Taurus

A Taurus, just like Aries, does not easily trust people when it comes to judgments. But on the contrary, a Taurus has more patience than Aries. It's just that Taurus wants proof. The Bull's pigheadedness makes Taurus suspicious of other people as well as their opinions. When somebody tells him something, he'll think about what it really means at the end of the day.

Gemini

This sign's flexibility make him find his feet in an environment. Gemini loves making others happy that he'll believe what they say just for the sake of it. He likes to feel accepted by the people around him. He seems gullible that he can believe people and their lies. Gemini needs to improve his sense of self so people won't lie to them easily.

SIX

Cancer

Cancer is an introvert so he's more likely to figure things out by looking inside himself. But the Cancer has the weakness to believe people very easily. It's for the reason that Cancer is quite lacking with self-confidence. What Cancer needs to do is to trust himself first before anyone else. With this, he'll be more powerful of his own mind and will eventually control his own life.

Leo

Leo, as a fire sign, believes people without too much questioning or analyzing. This makes Leo slightly unalike from fellow fire sign Aries. He will wholeheartedly trust in people. The fire makes him a very open and credulous person. With this, Leo has to believe in his own morals first so he won't be deceived by anyone.

VIRGO

Unlike most signs that are quite susceptible, Virgo differs in a way that he does not easily trust even in himself. He wants proof and that is a big factor for him to trust himself or other people. He is all about analyzing things before believing in them. He's quite critical and perfectionist that he often find fault with many things.

LIBRA

Libra, with his fair judgment, recognizes both sides to any argument. He will accept people as they are. He will not favor anyone because as much as possible, he likes to maintain that balance. His golden heart makes him consider that people are honest. He, however, should watch out for people who could use Libra's kindness to ask for help.

SCORPIO

Scorpio tends to be secretive that he thinks that he's alone. His sneaky nature will not make him trust people and anything they say. He trusts nobody. A Scorpio even lacks intellect when he is dejected. He could even scream out at the world. Thus, Scorpio has to go through deep stuff in order to appreciate others. He has to reflect in able to figure out who he needs to trust.

SAGITTARIUS

A Sagittarius loves life, so he believes that everything is all about opportunity and taking chances. He will not have a hard time trusting people. He trusts himself a lot that trusting other people will also be easy to him. Sagittarius just has to maintain that optimism and should not let anyone ruin his good spirit and good beliefs.

CAPRICORN

Capricorn is serious and sees life in black and white. He works, he gets paid. His own routine makes him happy. It's a sweat for him to go outside of the box to become outgoing. He does not believe in people that much. He will rather believe in himself than other people. Still, Capricorn should understand that trusting others will get them to a happier place.

AQUARIUS

This sign just loves to go with the flow. He has a strong enthusiasm for adventure and new experiences. He believes in life, he trusts in people. In turn, people also believe in him. He even believes in the overall goodness of people around him. Aquarius is an extrovert so it will be easy for him to express himself. He can make other people comfortable with him. In general, Aquarius dreams of freedom to live a happy and fulfilling life.

PISCES

Pisces, the last zodiac sign, has a heart for people. He loves to be around people but his suspicious nature will not let him trust others easily. However, a Pisces is a deep thinker that they are often tagged extremely unpredictable. It will be wise for a Pisces to learn to accept life as it is. He needs to trust in his own morals.

How Will Your Sex Life Be?

CAN astrology help you learn the secrets of your partner when it comes to sexuality? If you're trying to seduce your partner, it won't hurt to learn his preferences based on his zodiac sign. This final chapter will give you some cues how to seduce your guy or goal and make him or her fall under your spell.

Aries

This sign looks for spark when it comes to sexual love. And speaking of making love, an Aries is the type who likes to be pampered in bed. An Aries is fast and aggressive. His big confidence makes him sexy. He has very high energy levels so he likes to make love often, but briefly. It's because Aries is not concerned on the before and after. It's all because of his sense of urgency. An Aries also likes to be on top.

An Aries does not prefer too much foreplay. He wants to get right to the point. His head is his most erogenous zone, so he won't mind ending up with messy hair after making love. A scalp massage will turn him on and he'll eventually thank his lover in a sizzling way.

Taurus

The Bull is known for its lasting endurance in bed. A Taurus' stamina can produce smoldering marathons. Unlike Aries, he's in no rush, and he can enjoy foreplay even for hours. This sign is emotionally gentle yet physically tough. Since a Taurus has an intense need for security, he believes that it should go hand in hand with sexual fulfillment.

Unpredictability is a huge turn-off in bed. Even on sex,

Taurus can be possessive. He likes to take ownership of his partner. When it comes to making love, a Taurus uses all of his senses. Of all the signs, he's actually the most physical. He likes touching or smelling. Thus, an arousing massage is a big turn-on for a Taurus.

SEVEN

Gemini

Oral pleasures are a huge turn-on for a Gemini. He loves kissing and talking while making love. Even an intellectual conversation won't bother or interrupt him. It's because the biggest strength of this sign is his communication skills, this is all thanks to Mercury, the god of communication. Of all the signs, he's most likely to engage in phone sex.

Geminis also enjoy fantasy-sharing. They will love to hear you talking dirty or sending them dirty text messages. A Gemini prefers variety so he won't mind trying new sexual techniques and positions. He is also more driven by his intellect than his desire. He also loves engaging in playtime so it won't hurt to initiate a role-play to boost his libido.

CANCER

Cancer appears conservative in public, but he can be wild in bed. Once a Cancer breaks that outer shell, he will be really fun to be with. He's mysterious but he's got some sex fantasies rolling around his head. He can even surprise you with creative sexual positions.

He can get along with whatever makes his partner happy. He prefers his partner to be a bit aggressive in bed. But of all signs, he's least likely to participate in one-night-stands.

The Moon makes him emotional even in bed. He likes a certain degree of emotional involvement when it comes to making love. Even in bed, a Cancer's style is soothing and caring. He prefers positions wherein he can look into his partner's eyes.

To turn a Cancer on, bring him near the water. This water sign will appreciate a boat ride with a bit of strip off.

Leo

Leo loves attention so being treated as a god in bed seduces this fire sign. He'll be happy to see his partner sit onto his lap while he's sitting on the couch, grinding against his body.

Although he will take care of his partner in bed, the Lion's pride makes Leo want to be the best even in lovemaking. He will keep the passion and will avoid any tediousness. Leo aims for the wow-factor, so a quickie isn't a thing for him. He wants the appropriate foreplay at the right time and in the perfect setting. He takes sex seriously but it should be something entertaining.

VIRGO

Ruled by Mercury, a Virgo will appreciate meeting of the minds before the actual deed. He prefers a long-term sexual partner. He will take time to perfect his sexual technique to give his partner the best orgasm. Even while he is making love, he's still thinking of ways how to improve his performance in bed.

He likes to take control of the action so he'll appreciate a Lusty Lean position. He can be turned on by the idea that his partner is a slave. A Virgo likes to take charge in bed while still making sure that his partner is impeccably gratified.

LIBRA

Libra, as an Air sign prefers mental connection aside from physical connection. Talking about sex, the idea of give and take is very important for Libra; he likes to satisfy his partner and would love to be satisfied in return.

A Libra is ruled by Venus, the symbol of love and beauty, so it's a huge turn-on for this sign if his partner appreciates the finer things in life. A good dose of flattery and flirting seduces a Libra. Though, he may lack certainty even in the bedroom. It will be great for a Libra if his partner takes control.

SCORPIO

Scorpio, like Aries, is blessed with a naturally high libido. He is a sexual magnet that it will be hard to resist him. He has a legendary sexual stamina, so much so that making love with him will often be an unforgettable experience.

Once he's committed to a relationship, he can guarantee his partner sexual loyalty and devotion. Still, his complexity will remain even with his sexuality. A sense of mystery blows his mind.

. . .

SAGITTARIUS

For an adventure-seeking Sagittarius, sex is like a sport. He just likes to have fun in bed. He likes trying new positions even in crazy places.

Unlike Cancer, it does not have to be an intensely emotional experience. The Archer in him makes him love experimenting in bed. A surprise fast and furious quickie will turn on a Sagittarius. A new position will turn him on and challenge him.

CAPRICORN

Sex with a Capricorn does not have to be exotic or fancy. The Goat prefers simplicity so it will not be hard to turn him on. Though, love and sex should go together for this sign. He wants to feel that he is loved.

Like a Cancer, Capricorn is poised in public but can be a tiger in bed. Once a Capricorn trusts someone, he'll eventually show his massive appetite for sex. Something that makes him feel comfortable turns on a Capricorn. Giving him a sensual massage will surely make him horny.

AQUARIUS

Aquarius may not be as intense as other signs like Aries or Scorpio, but his open-mindedness makes him interested with sexual experimentation. He gets turned on by unfamiliar sexual encounters.

Ruled by Uranus, he has a need for variety in sex. He will be very happy to hear what turns his lover on. In return, he loves to whisper sweet nothings to his lover during thrust. Aquarius is game for phone sex. It just blows his mind.

PISCES

Seduction is the word for Pisces. Expect lots of sexual fantasies from this sign. Sex, for a Pisces, should be fun as well as creative. The Fish loves to be in the water so a skinny-dipping will blow his mind. He likes to experiment in bed. But like Cancer, he likes establishing emotional connection even when making love. He's also intense so he prefers a position wherein he can look at his partner's eyes.

AFTERWORD

I hope you enjoyed this book and that you were able to take some ideas from this book and apply them to your life.

I long for you to develop stronger connections with other people and to take your relationships to the next level, whether it be with improved friendships and understanding each other better or understanding sexual compatibility. Whatever it is, I hope you use and apply this new knowledge to your advantage!

www.ingramcontent.com/pod-product-compliance
Lightning Source LLC
Chambersburg PA
CBHW052129110526
44592CB00013B/1804